THE STORY OF VASCO DA GAMA

THE
STORY OF VASCO DA GAMA

M. T. YATES

GYAN

Published by

Gyan Publishing House
5, Ansari Road
Daryaganj, New Delhi-110002
Phone: 011-47034999, 9811692060
E-mail: books@gyanbooks.com

Distribution Network
gyanbooks.com
India, USA, Canada, UK, Australia, France

ISBN : 978-81-212-4071-0 (PB)
First Published, London

2nd Impression 2020

Printed at: Gyan Press, Delhi.

The
Story of Vasco Da Gama
Edited by: M. T. Yates

THE STORY OF

VASCO DA GAMA

Edited by M. T. YATES, LL.D.

LONDON
J. M. DENT AND SONS LTD.

PREFATORY NOTE

VASCO DA GAMA, a famous Portuguese navigator, was born about 1469. In his early years he distinguished himself as a daring mariner. After the return of Bartholomew Diaz, who had succeeded in doubling "the Cape of Storms," afterwards called the Cape of Good Hope, Da Gama obtained command of a small fleet to make further explorations in Eastern seas, and the first of these voyages is described in the following pages.

He sailed in 1497, doubled the Cape and crossed the Indian Ocean, arriving at Calicut in 1498. After a short stay he once more set sail and reached Lisbon in 1499. He went out to Calicut again in 1502 and in 1524, the last time with the title of Viceroy. He died at Cochin in 1524 and fourteen years later his body was taken home and buried with great pomp in his native country.

CONTENTS

ILLUSTRATIONS

CHAPTER I.

The Age of Discovery.

1. When Columbus made his famous voyage in 1492, he did not by any means achieve the object for which he set out. His purpose, in venturing on the perilous journey across an unknown ocean, was not to find a new continent, but a sea route to Asia.

2. It had long been thought that Asia, with all its rich gems, spices, and other treasures, might be reached by sailing westward from Europe. For hundreds of years there had been rumours of a land beyond the Atlantic, which, it was suspected, was no other than India. How to discover this supposed passage to India, had long been a puzzle before Columbus made his daring voyage.

3. The European nations, which had ships

and took pride in their commerce, were all anxious to be the first to find it. When Columbus, therefore, after passing safely through many perils, espied the lovely island of San Salvador, and afterwards Cuba and Hayti, he felt confident that he had made the long wished-for discovery, for which he would be envied the world over. He was perfectly sure that he had found Asia, and that India was not far off.

4. In the voyages he made afterwards, when he discovered Jamaica and the northern coast of what we call South America, he was still more convinced that a little farther search would bring him to the well-known shores of Hindustan. To his dying day Columbus believed that it was one side of Asia, and not a new land, that he had discovered. He was in so little doubt that it was India, or near it, that he had reached, that he called the people of the places where he landed, "Indians," a name by which we still know the early inhabitants of America.

5. It was not until some years had elapsed, after Columbus' travels had ended, that Europe found that he had struck on a

new and hitherto unknown continent. Meanwhile, the story of romance, adventure, and discovery he brought back, the accounts he gave of the beautiful islands and strange people and customs he had found far acoss the sea, and the great renown which by his voyage he had won, not only for himself, but for the good sovereigns, Ferdinand and Isabella, who had so generously aided him in his brave purpose, created the most lively excitement and sensation in Europe.

6. He was overwhelmed with honours, and in every part of Spain he was received as if he had been a great conqueror. Spain was very proud of his achievements, and the other nations were very jealous of the prestige and possessions, which she had obtained as the result of his success.

7. Among the other sovereigns to whom Columbus, some years before his discoveries, had in vain applied for aid in what then seemed his rash and foolish project, was John the Second, King of Portugal. Now, the little kingdom of Portugal had long been the rival of Spain in making discoveries. Indeed though she was far less rich and less

powerful than Spain, she had obtained greater triumph on the sea.

8. About eighty years before Columbus' first voyage, there lived in Portugal a brave and enterprising prince, named Henry. He was the fifth son of the reigning king, and, when young, had fought valiantly in the wars with the Moors. When peace returned to his country, Henry, who was an ardent student of geography and astronomy, instead of idling away his time at his father's court, spent it in encouraging and fitting out expeditions of discovery.

9. He had himself visited the northern countries of Africa. One reason why he turned his attention to voyages was, that he was anxious to find out whence the Moors got so much gold dust and ivory, and which, they told him, came from beyond the desert. It is said that the expedition, which Henry sent to explore the western coast of Africa in 1412, was the very first voyage of discovery undertaken by a modern nation.

CHAPTER II.

The Cape of Good Hope.

1. Among the discoveries made under the direction of Prince Henry of Portugal were the Canary and Cape Verde Islands, and various countries on the west coast of Africa as far down as Lower Guinea. In some places they found gold dust, ostrich feathers, and ivory, and other articles of great value. The ships brought home strange stories of the negroes, as well as rich merchandise.

2. The passion for discovery did not cease in Portugal with the death of Prince Henry, which occurred in 1463. Under King John the Second, the Portuguese advanced still further southward, to the Congo River. All the land thus discovered on the African coast was taken possession of in the name of the King of Portugal, and attempts were made to colonise them with his subjects. These attempts, were, in many instances,

successful. With the negroes on the African coast a brisk trade sprang up, and the fame of Prince Henry, as the "father of discovery," became a household word in his own country and throughout Europe.

3. King John, the same who refused aid when Columbus asked him, was yet resolved he would find out, if possible, a way to reach India by sea. He had heard that there was a rich and powerful king in India, called Prester John, who was a Christian. He thought it would be of great advantage if he could communicate with him and secure his friendship.

4. He accordingly selected two of his most trustworthy courtiers and told them to travel, as best they could, towards India by land, and see if they could find Prester John. The two young men set out, and going by way of Florence and Alexandria, arrived safely at Aden ; here they separated, agreeing to meet again at Cairo.

5. King John never heard of his two faithful explorers again. The accounts of India, which kept coming to him, however, inspired him with fresh exertions to reach

that land of fabulous wealth. Despairing of accomplishing this by a land route, he turned his attention to the discovery of a way to India by sea. It was thought that such a way might be found south of Africa.

6. The King accordingly fitted up an expedition, and chose Bartholomew Diaz, an officer of the royal household and a vigorous and intrepid man, to command it. Diaz set sail in 1486, and, after encountering many perils, succeeded in doubling the southernmost point of Africa. So frightful were the tempests which raged there, that Diaz named this southernmost point "the Cape of Storms."

7. When he returned to Portugal, however, and told King John of his discovery, the latter, in his delight, exclaimed that, since it held so bright a promise of reaching India by sea, it should rather be called the "Cape of Good Hope," which is the name it bears to this day.

8. A strange incident took place in this voyage of Diaz. In one of the most terrific storms his ship was separated from the vessel which accompanied him, and which

carried the provisions for his crew. At this the men grew desperate, fearing that they would be starved. They threatened to mutiny, unless Diaz should retrace his way home. Diaz, however, persisted, and doubled the Cape.

9. Returning homeward, he fortunately fell in with the vessel again. But, alas! of the nine men whom he had left in it, only three survived, such had been their sufferings from cold and hunger. So overjoyed was one of the survivors to see the ship again, that he fell dead at the captain's feet.

10. It was eight years after the discovery of the Cape of Good Hope by Bartholomew Diaz, that Columbus returned with his wonderful story of the discovery of America. This filled the Portuguese not only with admiration, but with great alarm lest Spain should get ahead of them in finding a sea route to the riches of the East.

11. They had every reason to be proud of their daring exploits as navigators. Columbus' story only inspired King John with a new resolve to seek a way to India by water, not westward, as the intrepid Columbus had

done, but around the Cape of Good Hope. He longed to win for Portugal the honour and riches which she would gain if her ships were the first to reach India, and he was determined to spare neither money nor energy in achieving this exploit.

12. Such a voyage was certain to be full of perils and difficulties, and many people in Portugal declared it was wicked to attempt it. They declared that the storms, which Diaz had encountered near the Cape of Good Hope, were constant, and that no ships could ever pass through them without foundering, or being cast on the shore, where the voyagers would soon meet with a terrible death at the hands of savages and cannibals. The King was implored by his nobles and subjects to abandon the project. It is greatly to his honour that he persevered in spite of so much eager opposition.

13. After sending out a foreign merchant to coast along Africa and take soundings—giving him many copper bracelets, looking-glasses, knives, silks, basins, rattles and bells, to give to the negroes, and so make friends with them—the King ordered his

workmen to build three large ships. Wood was cut in the forests, and brought to Lisbon, and the ships that were to undertake the great and dangerous voyage round Africa were forthwith begun.

14. Unhappily, just at this time King John fell ill, and, after lingering for several months, died without having experienced the joy of seeing his darling project brought to a conclusion. It was fortunate for the Portuguese that he was succeeded by a monarch, whose desire to conquer the ocean was not less intense than that of King John. It was under King Emmanuel, who now came to the throne, that the thrilling adventures and heroic exploits of Vasco da Gama took place.

CHAPTER III.

Vasco da Gama Sets Sail.

1. King Emmanuel lost no time in carrying out the plans of the late monarch. The three vessels were quickly completed and furnished with all necessary stores. Provisions, medicines, and a great variety of merchandise for trading purposes, were put on board.

2. Then Vasco da Gama, a young nobleman who had already done good work for his country, was chosen to command the expedition. His brother, Paulo, and his friend, Nicholas Coello, were selected by him to command the other two vessels. Vasco sailed in the "San Raphael," Paulo in the "San Gabriel," and Coello in the "San Miguel."

3. On a bright Sunday morning in the spring of 1497, the quaint, narrow streets and spacious squares of Lisbon were full of people. Something unusual, evidently, was

going forward. The old town had the aspect of a holiday, and the multitude, gaily dressed, were all flocking in the same direction.

4. In the square, where stood the ancient and stately cathedral, the crowd was most dense and most eager. Within the building itself a large assembly, composed of grandees and nobles, as well as the common people, filled every corner.

5. Behind a curtain, which separated them from the rest of the assemblage, the young King and Queen of Portugal, surrounded by a select few of the highest officers of the court, had taken their places. Near this curtain were Vasco and Paulo da Gama and Nicholas Coello, attired in rich and showy dresses, "the observed of all observers."

6. The voice of the Bishop of Lisbon alone broke the deep silence that reigned in the cathedral. When he had concluded his prayers, the Bishop turned to the assemblage, and told them to pray to God that the voyage of Vasco da Gama might be successful.

7. The service over, King Emmanuel came out from behind the curtain and spoke to the three captains, who knelt before him, and the courtiers gathered in a close group round them. The whole party then repaired from the cathedral to the royal palace, being cheered and saluted on the way by an immense concourse of people.

8. The time had now come to embark, and soon a procession was formed to proceed to the ships. Vasco da Gama, having kissed the hands of the King and Queen, mounted a fine Arab horse, and put himself at the head of the procession. By his side rode Paulo and Nicholas. Behind them marched, two and two, the crews of the ships, handsomely attired in uniform.

9. A large number of noblemen, and officers of the court, accompanied them. Throughout the route multitudes of people were gathered, many of them weeping at the perils their relatives or friends, the sailors, were about to encounter, others blessing and cheering them on with loud voices.

10. Arrived at the wharf, where the ships

lay moored, they found them gaily decked out with flags. When Vasco da Gama appeared, the firing of guns welcomed him to the command of the little fleet. The streets and houses near the wharf were occupied with a dense and excited crowd, who filled the roofs and balconies, and were closely packed together down to the water's edge. So many of the people were observed weeping and lamenting, that this place was afterwards called the "Shore of Tears."

11. Vasco da Gama sprang lightly from his horse, crossed the plank with stalwart step, and went on board the "San Raphael," followed by the sailors. In another minute his resolute face appeared on the deck, gazing on the familiar scenes to which he was about to bid adieu. His brother, Paulo, and Nicholas, also repaired on board their ships with their men.

12. Vasco, seeing that all was ready, gave the signal for departure. And now there was seen a busy stir on the decks, while the multitudes on shore remained breathlessly silent. The sails were spread as if by magic. The anchors were drawn up drip-

VASCO DA GAMA SETS SAIL

ping from the bottom. The cannon on the quay boomed forth a noisy "God speed!" The people shouted and waved their hands, to which Vasco and his comrades responded warmly from the decks. The three ships, looking gay, sturdy and gallant in the sunlight, floated smoothly out of Lisbon harbour.

13. The wind being contrary, the fleet proceeded no farther the first day than the little harbour of Belem, a few miles westward of Lisbon. Here they anchored till the breezes should be favourable.

14. Finally, on the third day, a good wind sprang up, and at last Vasco da Gama was fairly off. The King accompanied the ships in his barge as far out as the open ocean, where he took leave of the captains, and watched them till the tops of their masts had faded out of sight beyond the horizon.

CHAPTER IV.

St. Helena.

1. Fair winds and a quiet sea, blue sky overhead, and a mild and delightful temperature, sped the adventurers on their way. Vasco's spirits ran high. The songs of the crew, as they went about their work, betrayed the gaiety of all on board. The three ships and the provision bark kept well together. Often they were so near one another, that the captains could speak from vessel to vessel.

2. For a week they sailed on, until they were rejoiced to perceive land, which they soon recognised as the Canary Islands. So far, all was well ; they were on the right path. Little did they foresee the dangers through which they would have to pass, ere they reached their far-off destination.

3. Those dangers began, indeed, soon after the Canaries had disappeared from

their view. A violent tempest burst upon them, and for hours they were tossed about at the mercy of the waves. When the storm subsided, the "San Raphael," Vasco da Gama's ship, could not be seen anywhere by the others. A dreadful fear took possession of Paulo da Gama and Coello, lest their brave commander had foundered. Yet they persevered on their course, making directly for the Cape Verde Islands, as Vasco had commanded in case they were separated.

4. A week of doubt was ended by the arrival of the ships at Cape Verde, where they were gladdened by the sight of Vasco's standard floating in the breeze, and the gallant commander himself standing on the deck. The meeting was celebrated by the blowing of trumpets and the firing of cannon.

5. The ships now proceeded together to the little island of San Jago, one of the Cape Verde Islands, where they came to anchor in a snug inlet, and rested there for a week. They seized the occasion to take in fresh water, replenish the ships

with provisions from the bark, and repair the rigging and spars that had been injured by the tempest.

6. A month had now passed since they left Portugal. It must have been about the first of May when the ships sailed out of the San Jago bay, and turned their prows, as nearly as Vasco could guess, directly towards the Cape of Good Hope.

7. Vasco da Gama was full of courage as well as energy. He might have crept timidly along the African coast, and thus delayed his voyage for the sake of being more safe. But he was eager to reach and double the Cape, and to see what he could discover in the unknown seas beyond. He therefore stretched at once across the Gulf of Guinea, and held a straight course southward, making long tacks in that direction.

8. After leaving San Jago, several months elapsed before the eyes of the voyagers were again gratified by the sight of land. Sometimes the sailors became impatient, and were inclined to give up in despair. Sometimes they were deluded by what

seemed to be land, but which turned out to be a fog or a cloud on the horizon. Sometimes Vasco da Gama, consulting his compass, feared lest he had gone wide of his track. Sometimes frightful tempests threatened to submerge them all in the raging seas.

9. Still, week after week, and month after month, Vasco da Gama kept resolutely on his course. He had a quick temper, and when the sailors timidly suggested turning back, he warmly told them that they should go forward until they reached India, or till the sea engulfed them.

10. It was late in August when this long voyage across the ocean brought them at last to the southern coast of Africa. The days, they perceived, had become very short. Scarcely six hours of daylight enabled them to search for land on the east. Then the temperature, after being for a time insufferably hot, had become very cool again.

11. One morning, land came in sight, and the ships, which had been able to

THE FIGHT AT ST. HELENA BAY

keep in sight of each other all this time, ran down on the coast in the hope of finding a harbour. In this they did not at first succeed; but, sailing along the coast a little farther, they reached a bay, where they cast anchor. They named it St. Helena Bay, and Vasco da Gama was sure they could not be far from the Cape of Good Hope.

12. While at St. Helena Bay, Vasco tried to obtain some information from the natives about the Cape of Good Hope, but in this he did not succeed. Veloso, one of Vasco's men, visited a native village, where he was well received. He, however, acted foolishly and brought about an attack by the natives, in which Vasco was wounded by an arrow, but no lives were lost.

CHAPTER V.

Vasco da Gama Doubles the Cape.

1. About the 1st of September the sails were once more spread, the anchors weighed, and the vessels sailed seaward. A south-west breeze carried them swiftly along; and, Vasco having told his men in a confident tone that he was certain that the Cape was not far off, the little fleet set off cheerily on its way round the continent.

2. Scarcely had they emerged from the tranquil harbour of St. Helena, when the ships were struck by contrary winds and stormy weather. The waves soon rose to a great height, and tossed the poor little vessels about as if they were playthings.

3. The sailors trembled lest the furious waters, which they saw raging far above them on every side, should engulf them forever in the deep. The pilots could not

shout loud enough to make their voices heard, so deafening was the roar of the storm.

4. After brief periods of daylight, a long and dreadful darkness would hang over them, and prevent their seeing in what direction they were going. The ships drifted whithersoever wind and waves compelled them. It was now that the heroic resolution, courage, and constancy of Vasco da Gama were put to the test.

5. When the storm lulled for a time, his sailors, wearied and despairing, crowded round him, and passionately besought him to give up his purpose, and turn back towards home. They begged him to consider that these were the constant storms, which had always forbidden ships to pass the Cape. They cried out that, unless he turned back, they would all find watery graves. They declared that the land, which came in sight as often as they tacked to double the Cape, had no end, but extended to the Antarctic Sea.

6. But Vasco da Gama was not to be moved. At first he chid his men gently, and said to them,—

"I assure you, good fellows, the Cape is very near. Do not despair. If we keep tacking, we shall surely double it."

7. He set them a good example by freely sharing their hardships and dangers. Promptly, at the sound of the boatswain's whistle, Vasco da Gama appeared on the deck with the others. He seemed never to take any repose, often remaining day and night at the helm. He ate the same coarse fare that was allotted to the humblest sailors, and, when the pilot was exhausted, Vasco himself took his place.

8. Finally, however, he lost patience, and grew very angry at the pleading of the men. Gathering them all on deck, he sternly told them that he would stand out to sea until the Cape was doubled.

9. They had been making as many tacks to the windward as the storm would permit. Every time they returned again towards land they were disheartened to see the long and irregular coast reappear in the east. At last Vasco da Gama resolved he would make a long tack, and stand on it till it was certain that he could double the land.

10. After a few days, Vasco ordered the helmsmen to steer once more towards the continent. As they slowly sped south-eastward, prayers from all the decks went up to heaven, and both captains and men seemed to take more heart The sea grew calmer, and through the long nights and brief days the brave little vessels, showing each other coloured lights at intervals, so as not to part company, kept steadily on.

11. This time no land appeared, and Vasco da Gama ordered the ships to sail freely once more, in order, if possible to espy it. One morning they woke to find themselves floating on a tranquil sea, with a gentle wind wafting them forward. It was a pleasant morning, very unlike the many wretched, dismal days that had passed. Now, though they had seen no land, Vasco knew that they had doubled the Cape.

12. The two other ships were signalled to come near the "San Raphael," and the glorious news was shouted from deck to deck. Both captains and sailors gave themselves up to the most eager demonstrations of joy. Some climbed the masts and waved

their caps to each other from ship to ship. Some ran and got trumpets, which sent a joyous din over the serene and sunny sea. And some wildly embraced each other, and danced about on the decks.

13. All the dangers and troubles of the past were forgotten in a moment. As Vasco da Gama, his handsome face flushed with triumph and pleasure, strode up and down among his men, they kissed his cloak, and prayed for his pardon and showered blessings on him. They little knew that it would not be long before the keenest despair would seize them, and incite them to make an attempt on their brave commander's life.

14. A solemn quiet suddenly succeeded the joyful noise of shouts, singing, cannon, and trumpets. Arrayed in their robes, the priests appeared on the decks. With one accord every man dropped on his knees, pulled off his cap, and bent low his head; and then, amid the stillness, the solemn voices of the priests were heard, uttering to God the gratitude with which the hearts of all were filled to overflowing.

CHAPTER VI.

Mutiny.

1. After entering several bays, and finding nothing to satisfy their curiosity, or make it profitable to land, the vessels put out to the open sea again. In the daytime they ran under full sail as long as the wind would permit them, while at night they proceeded more slowly and cautiously. More than once they were becalmed, and had to lie by till a breeze sprang up. As they drifted farther away from the continent, they began to find that they had by no means left the storm region behind, when they doubled the Cape.

2. It was now winter. The voyagers were yet far from their destination, but how far they knew not. The sudden storms of that season of the year were not tardy in assailing them. One morning a terrific storm burst, almost without warning, over their heads. Vasco da Gama took his place on deck, and scanning the heavens with his keen eye, gave his orders rapidly and clearly.

3. Cheerily the men set about the tasks commanded by their captain; but, as they laboured, the tempest grew yet more furious. At last the pilot, doffing his cap, came up timidly to Vasco, and said,—

"I fear that the ships are not strong enough to weather this tempest, captain. Let us put in to land, run along the coast, and find a secure haven till the storm is past."

4. "No!" cried Vasco. "Return to your post, pilot! When I came out of Lisbon harbour, I swore not to turn back a span's breadth." The crew looked at him aghast, but his countenance was stern; they could find in it no sign that he would relent.

5. The gale was all this time increasing, and fitfully veered in every direction. The waves were running at a frightful height, and, falling, drenched the decks with floods of water. Then the wind suddenly lulled, so that the ships lay helpless in the surging sea, and lurched so badly, that they took in water on either side.

6. The men were forced to tie themselves

fast to the masts and rigging to save themselves from being washed overboard. It became almost impossible to work at the pumps. The ships creaked so noisily, that it seemed as if they might go to pieces at any moment.

7. The sailors now became more piteous in their appeals to Vasco to turn back; but he grimly replied,—

"I have said I would not. If I saw a hundred deaths staring me in the face, I should go straight on. To India we shall go or perish." Then he added, in more persuasive tones, "Think of the honours and rewards that our good King will shower on us when we return with the story of our exploits! Come, my men, pluck up courage, and put your faith in God."

8. It happened that, when the little fleet set out from Lisbon, five or six men who had been condemned to death for various crimes were released and put on board. The object of this was that Vasco da Gama might use these convicts to explore dangerous places, and thus not risk the lives of his sailors. The lives of the criminals were

looked upon as useless, and if they were killed by savages it mattered little.

9. These men, when they saw the crews give themselves up to despair in the midst of the tempest, and Vasco da Gama resolute in his purpose to go forward, thought it a good opportunity to make mischief. They got together at the end of the "San Raphael," and began to whisper among themselves. Presently, calling some of the sailors to them, they muttered mysteriously in their ears.

10. Just then the tempest lulled a little, so that the three ships could approach within speaking distance of one another. The sailors on the "San Raphael" began to shout to their comrades on the "San Gabriel" and "San Miguel," and to incite them to resist the orders of the captains. Vasco da Gama thereupon cried out to his brother Paulo, and to Nicholas Coello, that he would on no account turn back to the coast, and told them to keep bravely on their course.

11. A plot was really in progress, but it was defeated by the prompt action of the

brave leader of the expedition. Vasco made the leaders of the mutiny prisoners, and declared his intention of keeping them in irons until the ships returned to Portugal.

12. This firm conduct completely quelled the rebellious dispositions of the crews, who hastened to crave the captain's pardon for their mutinous designs. They begged him to release the men in irons, but, to this he turned a deaf ear. He took up his station at the pilot's place, and himself undertook to guide the ship on its perilous way.

13. When the other two ships again came near, Vasco da Gama told Paulo and Coello what he had done. The crews of the "San Gabriel" and the "San Miguel," disheartened by the failure of the crew of the "San Raphael," and won, moreover, by the gentle words of their own captains, who sought to persuade them from their design, soon gave up all thoughts of violence. So the little fleet sailed once more peaceably over the waters.

14. The long storm had meanwhile greatly damaged the three ships. Their holds were so full of water that the pumps

VASCO REFUSES TO RELEASE THE MEN

seemed to make little impression on the flood that had gathered in them. In many places the ships leaked, and betrayed sore need of repairs. The supply of fresh water for drinking had got very short, and the cooks were obliged to use salt water for cooking the provisions.

15. Vasco da Gama was prudent as well as brave. He saw the necessity of making land, if possible. He therefore ordered the ships to turn once more towards the African coast. It was not long before land came once more in sight, much to the delight of the crews. They passed close to a high and jagged rock, which Vasco called "the Rock of the Cross"; and on Christmas Day they skirted a cape, which he christened "Natal."

16. About ten days after this, Vasco da Gama espied the mouth of a large river, and a spacious bay well sheltered from the winds. Here he decided to cast anchor. So grateful were they all to find themselves floating in smooth waters, and near the land, that they called the stream "the River of Mercy."

CHAPTER VII.

The King of Melinda.

1. Vasco da Gama remained at the mouth of the River of Mercy several weeks. The vessels were all carefully examined, and, as the "San Miguel" was in very bad repair, it was broken up, and its crew and stores divided among the other two vessels, both of which were thoroughly refitted.

2. Having again put to sea, Vasco met with a large canoe not far from the shore. In this vessel he found a Moor, named Devane, who agreed to accompany him on his voyage, and who became one of his most faithful attendants.

3. Towards the end of March the vessels entered the channel between Madagascar and the African coast. Reaching the island of Mozambique, Vasco cast anchor in the harbour. Opening communication with the shore, he received a visit from the Sheik, who appeared very friendly. Finding, how-

ever, that a plot was being formed to seize his ships, he sailed away.

4. Late in April, the vessels arrived off the town and island of Mombasa ; but here Vasco met with the same treachery and craft which had caused him to depart suddenly from Mozambique. The Moors of Mombasa were found to be in league with those of Mozambique to destroy the vessels.

5. Proceeding along the coast, he came to Melinda, where both the king and the people presented a most favourable contrast to those already visited. Here he met with generous treatment, and was set fairly on the way to India.

6. It was on a bright, sunny morning that Vasco and Paulo set out in one of their large boats to go near the shore, and there hold an interview with the King of Melinda. The waters of the roadstead glistened in the sun's rays. The town was all alive with gaily-dressed people, who thronged along the quays, and covered the reef with a dense and excited mass. The walls of the town, the vessels and the ships anchored near, were gay with flags fluttering in the

light breeze. The country round was clothed in the luxuriant green and ample foliage of the African spring time.

7. The two boats, as they started away from the ships, were a sight to behold. Vasco and Paulo, attired in cloaks of crimson satin, with plumed caps and swords, sat on chairs covered with crimson velvet. Beneath their feet were spread brilliantly-coloured carpets. Over the sides of the boat hung woollen rugs, on which sat the men who had been chosen as the attendants of the two captains. Each boat carried two cannon, loaded, and pointed outward, and from each floated the royal flag of Portugal.

8. They rapidly rowed to the edge of the quay. There stood the old king, with his long, sweeping white beard, surrounded by his swarthy court, waiting to receive them. Vasco and Paulo rose from their chairs and saluted him with low bows and uncovered heads. An immense crowd of Moors and Arabs observed them from every point of view, and greeted them with loud acclamations.

9. They were still too far off, however,

to enable the king to converse with them. So he ordered his men to take him to Vasco's boat. Here a chair was placed for him, and Vasco, kneeling, made signs for him to sit. Paulo, having gone into his brother's boat, and the African slave who spoke Arabic being in attendance as interpreter, the king and the two captains soon engaged in an animated talk.

10. "Sire," said Paulo da Gama, whom his brother asked to speak, "we are deeply grateful for the honour you do us at this moment. We are anxious to be your friends and servants. We shall be bounden to you if it pleases you to establish peace and friendship with our liege lord, the King of Portugal."

11. "God knows," replied the king, "that I have already resolved on this in my heart. It is what I pray for and greatly wish. I will maintain, as long as I live, a brotherhood with your sovereign."

Vasco, on this, knelt and kissed the king's hands; but he raised him up again. And now the crews shouted out, "Welcome, O king! The Lord be praised."

VASCO VISITS THE KING OF MELINDA

12. The trumpets then were sounded, and the deep booming of the cannon was heard. The people on the shore were astonished at the noise, and pressed forward to listen to the unwonted sound.

13. Vasco da Gama now approached the king, and offering him a magnificent sword, the scabbard of which was enamelled with gold, a lance of gilded iron, and a buckler of crimson satin, sewn with gold thread, said,

"It is the custom, sire, for our king to present arms to any new friend or brother whom he adopts. These are given that you may defend yourself with them from all enemies. The sword is a token of knighthood, the greatest of earthly honours. Whoever breaks a friendship established by a gift of a sword, loses his honour for ever. Therefore, sire, we give you this sword and these arms in the name of our king; and we promise to always maintain with you sincere peace and friendship."

14. "I promise and swear by my faith," replied the king, "to always keep peace and friendship with my new brother of Portugal. This I say before all my people."

CHAPTER VIII.

The Faithful Moor.

1. Vasco was now convinced that the King of Melinda was sincere, and did not meditate any treachery or snare against the Portuguese. He no longer hesitated when the king sent him a second invitation to come on shore.

2. The next day, therefore, he proceeded to the quay, attended by twelve of his men handsomely dressed. He was received by a number of courtiers, who at once conducted him to the royal palace. At the door he was welcomed by the king himself, who embraced him, while Vasco kneeled, and saluted the king with a low bow.

3. His royal host conducted him within, and invited him to sit beside him on a raised daïs covered with silk. Here the conversation of the day before was continued, the interpreter standing respectfully below the daïs.

4. The king told Vasco that he had better not go to Cambay, but to some other port of India.

"The things you seek are not to be found in Cambay," he said; "or, at least, they cost much there. But I will give you pilots who will conduct you to the great city of Calicut. Near there grow pepper and ginger, and all other drugs are brought there from every clime. Your broker Devane must go with you. He knows the price of everything, and so you will not be cheated."

5. To all that the king said, Devane, who had come with Vasco, nodded assent. The king then turned to the Moor, and asked him if he would not continue his voyage with the Portuguese to Calicut. Devane replied, without hesitation,—

"Sire, I should rejoice to go to Calicut, or, for that matter, the world over with the Portuguese. I have seen much of them, and have been long in their company. They have treated me excellently well. And I know that the captain is generous, and will abundantly reward me."

6. "Assuredly I will," returned Vasco,

thanking the faithful Moor; "and so well that, wherever the Portuguese go hereafter, in these regions, people will hasten to serve them. And I promise you, sire, that on my return from India I will come here to tell you all that has happened to us, that you may rejoice with us in our good fortune, and share in our grief if our fortune is ill."

7. Vasco then apprised the king that the ships had fallen short of biscuits, and asked if wheat, which was used to make them, was to be had in Melinda. The king not understanding what was meant by "wheat," a boat was sent to the "San Raphael" to get some.

8. When he saw it, the king said that there was none grown in that country, but that the Cambay merchants brought a little of it to Melinda to be used for the royal table, and that as much as could be found Vasco should have.

"I wish it, sire, as soon as possible," said Vasco, "as I am anxious to start without delay."

9. "That you cannot do for three months," said the king; "you must wait at

least so long before you can cross the Indian Ocean."

"Why so?" asked Vasco in astonishment.

10. "Because the winds will not be favourable for you till then. You must sail with the monsoon, or trade winds. They are now contrary, blowing from the east. It will be three months before they shift round and set in from the west. At this season there are fearful storms, and you would surely be lost. It is most dangerous to cross the ocean in the face of the contrary trade winds."

11. This unwelcome piece of news was a surprise to Vasco, who was extremely chagrined to find that he must lose so much time, and postpone his longed-for arrival in India to so late a period. He had not heard of the trade winds, and this new obstacle, while it did not discourage him, made him sad and anxious.

12. Bidding his royal host adieu, he returned to the "San Raphael," and found, when he got there, a new proof of the king's generosity and goodwill. A boat had been

sent out, not only with big copper kettles full of boiled rice, but also a number of sheep roasted whole, some excellent butter, wheat and rice cakes, some boiled and roasted chickens, vegetables, figs, cocoanuts, and sugar canes.

13. There was enough for all the crews, as well as the captains and officers. While Vasco, Paulo, and Coello sat down to a table groaning with good things, the men feasted on deck right merrily. Vasco hastened to send the king, in return, some preserved pears in silver basins, and a fork to eat them with, first eating some of the pears in the presence of the king's servant to show that they were not poisoned.

CHAPTER IX.

Waiting for the Trade Winds.

1. Vasco informed his brother captains of what he had learned from the king, and they all deplored the necessity of waiting so long a time at Melinda. They feared that the king's disposition towards them might change, and that false and hostile stories might reach him from Mombasa and Mozambique. In order that this might not happen, they resolved that none of the sailors should go on shore except the sick, who needed change of scene and occupation; and that the Moor, Devane, should be told to remain always with the king, so that he might contradict any evil stories that might reach their royal friend.

2. Calling Devane to him, Vasco said,—

"I pray you go to the king, and be always near him. While you are there, no Moor will dare to speak evil of us. The Moors of the coast, no doubt, are jealous lest we become their rivals in trade, and will do all they can to poison the king's mind against us. Since we are forced to stay here so long, it is best to foster the friendship which the king now shows us.

3. With this the Moor, smiling, said to Vasco,—

"Captain, how is it that, I being a Moor, you repose so much trust in me?"

"My heart tells me that you are a true friend," returned Vasco. "You have done us many good turns, and never a bad one, and so I am led to confide in you." This pleased Devane very much.

4. Vasco was very grateful to the good Moor for his fidelity, and now showed his gratitude by throwing a heavy gold chain about his neck, which Devane, delighted, hastened off to show the king. The king, equally impressed with Devane's goodness, made him a present of a silken cloak. Obeying the orders of Vasco, the Moor took up his abode in the royal palace. The king grew very familiar with him, and, being a jolly old fellow, sat and joked with him by the hour together.

5. Meanwhile Vasco made the best of the situation, and prepared to wait at Melinda

till the trade winds became favourable. There was much, indeed, that might be done during the three months before them, and no lack of work and recreation to make the weeks pass rapidly.

6. Calling together the master and pilots, Vasco told them of the delay, and gave orders as to how the time was to be employed. The ships were in some need of repair, and it was necessary to get in provisions for a voyage which, should the weather prove unfavourable, might be long and tedious.

7. Once more the ships were heeled over, and the sides thoroughly caulked. The decks and upper parts were made watertight with pitch. Ropes were twisted of a thread made by the natives from the outer husks of cocoanuts, which proved to be excellent for the purpose, as they could be stretched like indiarubber, and were yet stronger in salt water than the cables brought by the Portuguese.

8. Vasco's wisdom, in making his sailors learn to be artisans before they left Lisbon, was now fully confirmed. Some of them

REPAIRING THE SHIPS

set to work making hawsers and rigging; others employed themselves on such carpentry work as the ships needed, inside and out; yet others proved to be skilful caulkers. Much of the work of making ropes and rigging was done on shore. This brought a crowd of curious Moors about the sailors every day.

9. At the same time, the work of provisioning the ships went actively on. They were supplied with an abundance of fresh water, which was obtained without difficulty from the streams near Melinda; meat, vegetables, meal, and fruit were brought on board, and stowed away for future use.

10. In this provisioning of the ships the Portuguese were greatly assisted by the king, who ordered a crier to go through the town to proclaim that nothing was to be sold to the strangers for more than it was worth. If any merchant overcharged them, the king declared that his house should be burned to the ground.

11. Vasco and his brother captains now went on shore fearlessly as often as they pleased. The king, remaining steadfast in

his friendship, would have them to dine with him, take them on excursions round the city and suburbs, and promenade with them in a large pleasure garden near the palace.

12. The time at length came for bidding the good old king and his fair city farewell. It was the 5th of August; and the 6th was the day appointed for the Portuguese to sail. In the afternoon a number of boats came out to the ships, fairly loaded with good things. There were great boxes of biscuit, rice, and butter, a quantity of boiled mutton, live sheep, fowls, and vegetables, cocoanuts, fruit, and sacks full of sugar. Such was the generous parting gift of the king.

13. Early the next morning he came out to the ships to bid them all good-bye. The old man was really overcome by the prospect of their departure, and embraced Vasco and Paulo, begging them not to forget to come that way on their return from India. As the royal boat slowly wended its way back to the shore, the trumpets sounded, the cannon roared, and the crews cheered, and shouted, "Lord God be with you, farewell!" Vasco and Paulo stood on the quarter-decks,

and waved their hands to the king, the people on the crowded quays and reef, and the crews of the ships which lay at anchor all round them.

14. Vasco, in a loud voice, gave the order to loosen the sails; and, with a fair wind blowing in the right direction (for the trade winds had now shifted, and were favourable), the "San Raphael" and the "San Gabriel" floated gaily out of the roadstead of Melinda.

15. They were about to stretch off into the vast and unknown ocean which lay between them and the crowning object of their perilous voyage. Until then, they had only been skirting the African coast, seldom losing sight of land, and constantly occupied by new sights and adventures. Now they were to brave the dangers of strange seas, filling the wide space of nearly two thousand miles between the shores of Africa and Asia.

16. Happily, in Vasco da Gama the ships had a cool commander with a clear head, and a strong, confident, and cheerful heart; and one and all looked forward with lively hope and cheerful expectation to the voyage before them.

CHAPTER X.

India at Last.

1. With what an eager, hopeful heart Vasco da Gama had set out on this voyage across the Indian Ocean! How long seemed the days in crossing it, and how vast seemed these uncertain seas! If he could only at last reach the welcome shores of India, the haven he had now been seeking, amid every danger, for nearly a year and a half; if he could make a treaty of friendship with the sovereign of that country, and load his vessels with its riches, with what a thrill of pride and joy would he turn his prows towards home.

2. How proudly would he enter the harbour of Lisbon with his precious cargoes and his glorious news! He would then be hailed, not only by his countrymen, but by all Europe, as the discoverer of the unknown passage which had been sought so long. He would be named as the equal and rival of Columbus. No honours would be too great

for his deserts. His exploits would go down in history, making his name for ever famous, and his deeds the admiration of remote generations.

3. We may well believe that these glowing thoughts filled the ambitious soul of Vasco da Gama as the friendly trade winds sped the "San Raphael" and the "San Gabriel" over the unknown ocean. Often, sitting on his quarter-deck, he gazed over the waters, as if yearning to behold the promised land of India.

4. Eagerly he listened to the words of the Melinda pilots as they assured him that they were on the right track, and that it would not be many days before the peaks of the Malabar mountains would gladden their sight. The two vessels were able, thanks to the favourable weather, to keep close together. Sometimes they were so near each other that Vasco could talk with his gentle brother, Paulo, from deck to deck.

5. Both the pilots and sailors were in the best of spirits. No thought of turning back, or of resisting the captain's will, seemed to enter their heads. Vasco spent much of his

time talking with the Moors on board through interpreters, and learning as much as he could from them of the people and land of India. Some of them had been there, and could tell him much that was interesting and valuable for him to know.

6. The voyage was, almost without interruption, a pleasant one. The trade winds blew the vessels steadily in the right direction. If a gale swept over the waters, it only served to carry them more rapidly on their way. Thanks to the thorough repairs which both ships had undergone, no accident or mishap occurred to either of them. Thus they went on day after day, no incident occurring to delay their steady progress, and nothing happening to vary the monotony of the voyage.

7. One morning, when the voyage had lasted about nineteen days, the Melinda pilot came to Vasco da Gama with an air of satisfaction on his grave, dark face and, pulling off his cap, said, —

"Captain, I am sure we are very near the coast of India. It would not surprise me if we should see land to-morrow morning."

8. Vasco's heart bounded in his breast at these words, and he uttered a profound thanksgiving to God. He thanked the pilot also, and promised that he should not regret it, should it turn out that he was a true prophet. Very likely the gallant captain did not sleep soundly that night. Early in the morning he was on deck with his men, and the eyes of all were straining towards the east, each eager to catch the first glimpse of land.

9. A number of sailors were perched in the main-tops as look-outs. Vasco was at his usual post on the quarter-deck. Suddenly a loud cry was heard from several mouths,—

"Land, land, land!"

10. A moment afterwards, the pilot came running up, and, prostrating himself at Vasco's feet, pointed with trembling finger at the horizon in the east.

"Behold, captain! the land of India!"

There was a confused shout of joy on both decks; wild cries of delight; a frantic rushing to and fro of sailors, some with tears running down their cheeks; a moment in

THE FIRST SIGHT OF INDIA

which there seemed no officers, no order on board, but in which Vasco, Paulo, Coello, the sailors, and the Moors, seemed to be simply a crowd of weary wanderers who now saw the goal of all their hopes.

11. Then the voice of the captain rose above the noise, and there was silence.

"There," he said, pointing eastward, "there is India! Let us first thank Heaven that has guided us hither."

12. So saying, Vasco da Gama fell on his knees, and all the rest followed his example. Not a word of prayer was spoken. The hearts bowed before God were too full for utterance, but it is certain that in every one Vasco's silent prayer was heartily echoed.

13. When the solemn thanksgiving was over, and they once more gazed eastwards, the great news was confirmed. There could be no doubt about it. What had been but a filmy streak, a faint, hazy line in the distance, had now grown into the substance of blue, though indistinct heights, rising apparently from the pale waters, and softly reflecting the rays of the bright sun.

14. Vasco da Gama, grateful to the

Moorish pilots for their fidelity, called them to him, and gave each a robe of red cloth and a goodly sum of money, which they received with evident delight.

15. It was afternoon when the ships approached near enough for objects on shore to be seen, and the broad, shining beaches stretching away into the distance. They ran along the coast, and ere long came in sight of a good sized town, nestled in a bay, with thatched houses, and a number of fishing boats. The inhabitants seemed greatly surprised to see the ships, and the fishermen in their boats came quite near to examine them.

16. At first, Vasco da Gama mistook this town for Calicut, and was greatly disappointed to see so rude a place.

17. The pilot soon undeceived him.

"That place," he said, "is called Cananor. But be not discouraged, captain. Calicut, the great city, is only twelve leagues distant, to the southward."

CHAPTER XI.

Arrival at Calicut.

1. Meanwhile the ships ran along the coast southward; and that night Vasco da Gama went to bed, well assured that the next day he should at last see the famed city of Calicut.

So, indeed, it happened. The morning was fine, and the wind favourable. Before noon the city loomed before their eyes. Its domes and minarets glittered in the sunlight. Its broad quays seemed full of life. In the bay on which stood Calicut floated many ships from all parts of the East.

2. Vasco da Gama was, however, too wise to venture within the bay, or to cast anchor too near the shore. He was by no means sure of the reception he would meet with, nor would he venture to brave a possible hostility with his two frail little ships and his handful of men.

3. At the entrance of the bay was a small town, about six miles from Calicut. Here there was safe anchorage at a convenient distance from the city, and yet near enough to enable the boats to go easily to and from the coast.

4. It was now sundown, and Vasco da Gama thought it best to wait till morning before attempting to enter into any communication with those on shore.

Meanwhile he called together his brother Paulo, Coello, and the faithful Moor, Devane, and consulted with them how to deal with the King of Calicut.

5. At first, Vasco proposed to go himself on shore the next morning, to present himself before the monarch, and frankly tell him the purpose for which he had come to India. But Devane warned him by no means to do this, as the king might be hostile, and, if he were, no one could tell what he might do. The best way, Devane thought, was to first demand hostages for his safety, as this was the custom in the East.

6. The next morning, no sooner was the

sun fairly up than a number of boats surrounded the two ships. In them were Indians with dusky skins, and naked, except that they wore cloths of different colours round their loins. They seemed very curious to know who the Portuguese were, and whence they had come. The shore, too, was soon crowded with a multitude of people, who gazed at the two ships as if they were some unknown monsters of the deep that had suddenly appeared to them.

7. Among the boats were some fishing-smacks, and these came up close to the ships. Vasco ordered his men to call the fishermen, and offer to buy their fish. The Indian fishermen went on board at once, and were delighted to receive some silver coins in exchange for their wares.

8. The story of the strangers' arrival came to the ears of the King of Calicut, who was called the Zamorin. He told the fishermen to return to the ships, carrying figs, cocoa-nuts and chickens, and to find out all they could.

Presently a boat laden with wood to sell came up to the "San Raphael"; but, as there was plenty of wood on board, Vasco declined to buy it. The men in the boat were going away much disappointed, when Vasco had them called back, and ordered some money to be distributed among them.

9. Devane asked him why he did this.

"Because," replied Vasco, "they are poor men, and came to sell their wood, and were going off disappointed. So I gave them money, that their labour might not be lost. It is thus I am wont to treat with those who try to serve me."

The Indians were told this reply of the captain's, and, going ashore, repeated it to their people, which favourably impressed them with the Portuguese.

10. For three days nothing was done except engage in trade with the fishermen. On the fourth day, however, a large boat came out to the "San Raphael," bringing a man of high birth, whom they called a Nair—a messenger from the Zamorin.

11. This Nair was naked, except that he wore a white cloth about his loins. He carried a small, round shield, some wooden slings, and a short naked sword with an iron

hilt. His hair was matted close to his head. He was tall, well proportioned, and very dark.

12. He refused to go on board, but spoke to Vasco da Gama through an interpreter from his boat. His message from the Zamorin was to ask who the strangers were, and what they wanted in Calicut.

13. Vasco replied that he had not sent his message to the Zamorin, since he had not until now had his permission to do so. But he would send a messenger on shore with the Nair, who would answer the Zamorin.

14. The Moor, Devane, accordingly went back with the Nair, and, on being ushered into the king's presence, repeated the story Vasco da Gama had told him to tell. He said that the Portuguese had come from the greatest Christian king in the world, who had sent in peace and friendship to buy cargoes of pepper and drugs with the rich cloths, and gold and silver, which they had brought with them.

15. The Zamorin seemed much astonished to hear this, and began to talk earnestly with

his courtiers. Meanwhile one of his officers asked the Moor how he came to be with the Portuguese.

Devane told him; and added an account of the noble and generous presents which Vasco had given the King of Melinda. The Zamorin, it appeared, was very covetous, and, when he heard this, eagerly assured Devane that Vasco was welcome to Calicut.

16. "Tell him," added the monarch, "that I will fill his ships with as much pepper and as many drugs as he can carry away with him."

He then sent Devane back to the "San Raphael," taking good care to provide him with a present of figs and chickens for the captain.

17. The return of the Moor with the friendly messages greatly pleased the brothers, who rejoiced in the prospect of securing the Zamorin's goodwill, and of obtaining a valuable cargo with which to return to Portugal.

They regaled themselves with the provisions which the Zamorin had sent, and resolved to send Devane to him with other messages next day. Devane, accordingly, returned in the morning to the city, and told the Zamorin that the captain was unwilling to enter upon trading until he had made a secure treaty of peace. He begged the Zamorin to send hostages, so that the captain might go on shore and visit him in person, and deliver the letter he had from the King of Portugal.

18. Meanwhile the Zamorin, who had seemed so eager to welcome Vasco, had not only consulted with his advisers, but had become subject to a powerful influence which was brought to bear in hostility to the Portuguese. While Vasco da Gama slept in the serene confidence that his troubles were at an end, that he had already secured peace and friendship with the Zamorin, powerful enemies were working on the mind of the sovereign, and doing everything in their power to persuade him to send the Portuguese away.

CHAPTER XII.

Something about Calicut.

1. Calicut, at the time of Vasco da Gama's voyage, was one of the largest, richest, and most famous cities in India. Its fame had reached Europe, and it was known that there dwelt one of the most powerful monarchs in the East. Situated on the south-western coast of India, with a good harbour, it was the centre of a very active and prosperous trade.

2. Hither came the great Arabian and Egyptian merchants to seek for the precious spices, drugs, and other merchandise that India afforded. Hither, too, came the Hindus from the interior with the goods bought by the merchants, and sent even from distant Genoa and Venice.

3. Calicut was, and is, situated on a low,

flat country, with occasional high hills rising from the level, and overlooking the sea. It is said that the whole district round was once covered with water ; and there is a legend that the god of the waters caused the ocean to recede, and leave a large space, for the benefit of some devotees, who prayed for this favour.

4. Some centuries before Vasco's arrival, the Moors of Mecca, in Arabia, coasting about in their rude vessels, had discovered India, and had come as far as Calicut. They were an enterprising race, and finding the trade with India profitable, continued to visit the coast with many vessels for a long period of years, carrying cargoes to and fro. Gradually these Arabs began to settle at Calicut and other places on the coasts.

5. The trade between the Arabs and the Hindus included a great variety of precious and useful articles. In the warehouses of Calicut were to be found not only spices and drugs, but precious stones, musk, lacquer and earthenware, gold, amber, wax, and ivory, cotton and silk cloths, and cloths of gold, grain, carpets, copper, quicksilver,

vermilion, alum, coral, rosewater, preserves, and provisions in bewildering profusion.

6. The city was large enough to cover a space of several miles square. Its trade was so prosperous that many of the Arab and Moorish merchants, who resided there, owned as many as fifty ships ; and it was not rare for five or six hundred vessels to visit its harbour in the course of a single winter.

7. It has already been related that a man of high birth and military bearing, called a Nair, visited Vasco da Gama in the harbour, as the messenger of the Zamorin. The Nairs formed a distinct rank and caste in Calicut. They comprised the upper class of the people. They went almost naked and with bare feet, wearing only a painted cloth from the waist to the knees, and a small turban on their heads. For arms they carried bows and arrows, spears, daggers, and rude, short swords. They were a valiant and well disciplined body of men.

8. Calicut was composed mostly of straw huts, but there were many temples, pagodas, palaces, and Arab residences here and there, which were built of stone and lime, with

tiled roofs, and were several stories high. In the suburbs of the city were many delightful orchards and gardens, with palm groves and fruit trees, and wells of delicious water. The ships which were lying in the harbour were like those seen by Vasco da Gama on the African coast; built without nails, the planks and beams being fastened together with cords of the cocoanut fibre. The bottoms were flat, as there were no keels to the ships.

9. The rich and powerful Arab merchants of Calicut, had no sooner heard of the arrival of the Portuguese ships outside the harbour, than they began to be very much alarmed. They feared lest these Europeans should become their rivals in trade, if, indeed, they did not rob them of their trade altogether. They had now no rivals, and were waxing richer and richer by the commerce they were carrying on. They looked on the Portuguese ships as forerunners of the fleets, which would come from Europe and bear away the rich cargoes they themselves were in the habit of obtaining.

10. So the Arabs in Calicut met together,

and resolved to do what they could to poison the Zamorin's mind against the Portuguese, and to induce him, through fear, to send the ships away. They despatched messengers to the towns along the coast, and warned their brother Arabs of the danger which threatened their trade. Many of these Arabs hurried from these towns to Calicut to help their countrymen there to get rid of the Portuguese.

11. Among the Zamorin's officers was a treasurer, and a minister of justice who was called the "Gozil." These two men had no little influence over the sovereign, and being greedy and corrupt, they were both open to bribery.

12. The principal Arabs resorted, then, to the treasurer and the Gozil, and, making them promises of large sums of money, begged them to rouse the Zamorin's fears and suspicions against the strangers. They engaged them to tell him that the Portuguese, who were rich, had not come hither for the peaceful purposes of trade, but to make conquests of the rich Indian kingdom.

13. They also said that these ships had

been sent out as spies to see whether this could be done; and that, doubtless, unless they were ordered away, they would be followed by large fleets, which would come and attack the power of the Zamorin and other Indian princes.

14. The two officers listened to the Arabs, and pretended to be convinced by them. They gladly accepted the presents that the Arabs offered, and promised to tell the king what they said. But, when the officers were alone, they said to each other that they would be cautious, and not say all that had been said to them. They would say just enough to arouse in the Zamorin's mind distrust of the Portuguese, but would leave the way open to take another tack, if, after all, the Zamorin should find it profitable to make friends with the Portuguese, and treat them well. Meanwhile, they would get as many presents as possible out of the Arabs.

15. The Gozil went to the Zamorin, and said enough to make him somewhat wary and suspicious. The monarch, however, was so covetous of wealth, and so impressed by what the Moor, Devane, had told him of

the generous deeds of the Portuguese at Melinda, that he resolved to continue his dealing with Vasco da Gama.

16. The Zamorin was under the influence of what the Gozil had said to him, when the Moor, Devane, came to him a second time, as has been related. He therefore delayed his reply to the request for hostages, but bade Devane return to the ship, and tell the captain to send any one on shore whom he chose, to look at the city and make purchases, and to say that whosoever he sent should be allowed to go and come in safety.

17. Vasco da Gama was much put out to perceive that the Zamorin was suspicious. He had hoped that there would be no difficulty in making peace with him, and winning his confidence. However, he was resolved to make the best of circumstances, and in all ways conduct himself in such a manner as to banish distrust from the Indian monarch's mind. It was very important that he should, if possible, conciliate the Zamorin, and succeed in procuring a cargo, so as to show King Emmanuel, on his return, that his voyage had been successful.

18. On board the "San Raphael" was a man of unusual intelligence, who had been sentenced for some crime to banishment, but had been allowed to go with Vasco da Gama on his voyage. This man's name was Joan Nunez. Fortunately he understood both Arabic and Hebrew.

19. Vasco chose Joan Nunez to accompany Devane on shore, telling him to observe everything narrowly. He was to listen to all that the people said, but to be very cautious in answering any questions they might ask him. He warned Joan on no account to separate from Devane, but to keep always close to him. He also gave him some money, and a list of provisions that he wished him to buy, instructing him to purchase no other goods, but only to note what there was in the shops. The next morning, therefore, Joan Nunez and Devane went on shore in one of the boats, and prepared to obey Vasco da Gama's commands.

CHAPTER XIII.

Adventures at Calicut.

1. No sooner had Joan Nunez and Devane stepped on the quay than they were surrounded by so eager a crowd, anxious to see Nunez (for rarely had these people seen a white man), that they were almost smothered and could scarcely push their way through. Nunez had to keep a tight hold on Devane's cloak, so as not to get separated from him.

2. Devane, hurrying along, made his way as best he could to the Gozil's house. This great man received them warmly, and gave them permission to ramble freely through the city. Having heard how rudely they had been jostled by the people, he sent one of his servants to keep a clear passage.

3. As they passed along the streets, some of the Arab merchants saw them. These hastened to persuade the Gozil to retain Nunez and Devane in the city over night, so that they might be questioned and some-

thing might be learned from tnem that tne Arabs could use against the Portuguese. This the Gozil, remembering the presents of the Arabs, promised to do.

4. Joan and Devane were walking leisurely through a long street gazing at the low shops and bazaars, with their curious wares of ivory and fruit, when suddenly a man came up to them, and looking hard at Joan, to his great astonishment addressed him in Spanish.

5. The man asked him where he was going.

"We are going," replied Joan, "to sleep at the Gozil's house."

"I pray you do not," responded the man who had spoken Spanish, "but come along with me to my house."

6. But the Gozil's servant would not permit them to go until his master's consent was obtained. The Gozil, when appealed to, readily granted their request, and, when they reached the man's house, he made them welcome with a bounteous supper.

7. He asked them where the ships were from, and all about their adventures. He told

them that he himself was a native of Seville, in Spain. He went on to say that, when a small boy, he had been taken prisoner and brought to Asia by some Moors. On regaining his liberty, he wandered about a good deal, at last finding a home in Calicut. In order to save his life, he had adopted the customs of the Moors.

8. Joan begged his host to go with him next morning to the ships, where he would be sure of a hearty welcome from Vasco da Gama. The man, whose name was Monsayde, readily accepted the invitation. Early in the morning, having taken leave of the Gozil (for Vasco da Gama had strictly enjoined upon Devane to omit no ceremony of politeness), the three men went out in a boat to the "San Raphael."

9. As soon as Monsayde found himself on deck, he ran up to Vasco and Paulo da Gama, who were seated on the quarter-deck, and making a profound bow, exclaimed in Spanish,—

"Good luck, sirs! good luck! Many rubies, many emeralds! You are bound to thank God for bringing you to this port.

Here there is plenty of all sorts of spices, precious stones, and other riches."

10. Vasco's surprise at hearing him speak Spanish was as great as that of Joan had been, while the sailors and cross-bowmen, who had gathered round, were so much affected at hearing the familiar tongue of their Spanish neighbours, that some of them fairly wept for joy.

11. "Honoured Castilian," said Vasco in welcome, "God give you health!" Before long, Monsayde was on the best possible terms with the captain and the Portuguese. Vasco made him sit on a stool by his side, and tell him how he came to be in this remote country, and, dinner time having arrived, invited him to dine, which he did, sitting at one table with Joan Nunez, while the captains ate at another near by.

12. Then Vasco da Gama told Monsayde about the voyage, and the objects for which he had come, and asked if he thought that the Zamorin would prove friendly to him.

Monsayde listened as if he had something on his mind. He seemed troubled, and twitched about nervously on his seat.

13. At last he broke out, speaking as if with an effort, and said,—

"Listen to me, captain, for I have something to confess. When I came on board this ship, I had it in my heart to betray you. I came as a spy for the Arabs, your enemies, and was going to reveal to them all that I heard and saw. But you have treated me so kindly that I will truly be your faithful and devoted friend."

14. He went on to tell Vasco how the Arab merchants, jealous of the Portuguese, and fearing that the arrival of the ships boded no good to their trade, had conspired to have the ships sent away. They had bribed the Gozil and the treasurer to aid them by setting the Zamorin against the Portuguese. They had also promised Monsayde himself handsome gifts if he would come and pretend a friendship with the strangers, make himself acquainted with their affairs, and betray them.

15. "It was with this bad purpose," Monsayde went on, "that I invited your men to my house last night, and that I came on board this ship. But now I pray you, captain, command me what to do, and you

shall see that I am not false to you, though it is reasonable you should not trust me, since I appear among you in the guise of a Moor among Moors."

16. Vasco da Gama, however, accepted his offer of friendship, and presenting him with some green cloth, told him that his reward would be much greater if he proved trustworthy.

17. Vasco da Gama, having considered what Monsayde had said, announced to Paulo and Coello that, if the Zamorin invited him to visit him, he should boldly go and entrust himself in his hands. Against this the other captains warmly protested, and asked Vasco what would become of them if he should meet with foul play. They begged him to send some one else, who might represent that he was the captain, and so make terms with the Zamorin.

CHAPTER XIV.

Vasco da Gama Visits the Zamorin.

1. Vasco da Gama made his preparations to go on shore, and pay a visit to the swarthy sovereign of Calicut. He ordered the presents to be got ready, and twelve picked men to put on their best apparel to accompany him to the court in due state. The presents intended for the Zamorin were rich and curious.

2. Among them were red cloths and velvets, a piece of yellow satin, a chair covered with rich brocade and ornamented with shining silver nails, two cushions of red satin with gold thread tassels dangling at the ends, a chased and gilded hand basin and ewer, a large and richly gilded mirror, fifty scarlet caps with crimson twisted silk buttons and tassels, and fifty sheaths of Flemish knives with ivory handles.

3. As the boat bearing Vasco da Gama, his twelve guards, and the presents, pushed out from the "San Gabriel," it presented a gay and novel sight to the concourse of

Indians that crowded the quays. Flags and steamers fluttered at the bow and stern. Cannon peeped over the side. The rich apparel of the captain and his companions shone brilliantly in the sunlight.

4. On landing, Vasco da Gama dressed himself so as to appear worthily before the Zamorin. He put on a short tunic of blue satin, and a handsome enamel collar. Round his waist he tied a rich sash, in which was a gold handled dagger. Over all he wore a cloak of yellow satin lined with brocade, which reached to the ground. On his head he placed a blue velvet cap, adorned with a long white feather, and his feet were covered with white buskins.

5. Thus arrayed, Vasco da Gama went out of the warehouse, in front of which a procession was formed to go to the palace. By the captain's side walked a handsome young page dressed in red satin. In front of him walked his twelve guards, one behind the other, bearing the various presents, the one who carried the chair going first. On either side of the Portuguese proceeded a body of two hundred Nairs in military costume,

commanded by the captain of the Zamorin's guard.

6. In advance of the procession marched several Portuguese trumpeters, blowing their instruments with all their might. From the Portuguese boats moored in the harbour cannon were fired as the company set out. The crowd was so great along the route that it was with difficulty that the Nairs could keep it from pressing on Vasco da Gama and his men.

7. The crowd became so dense that they had to take refuge for a while in a house on the way till the streets were cleared. A large body of the Zamorin's troops now joined them, and they set forth again. As Vasco walked along and saw not only the streets, but the doors, windows, and roofs occupied by a closely packed mass of swarthy spectators, he exclaimed,—"They little think in Portugal with what honour we are received here!"

8. It was late in the afternoon when the procession reached the royal palace. Vasco found this to be a large and really handsome edifice, surrounded by pleasant copses of

trees, and gardens brilliant with flowers and adorned with fountains.

9. At the palace gate were a group of noblemen, richly attired, waiting to receive the Portuguese captain, and to conduct him to the Zamorin's presence. At their head was a little old man, who proved to be the head priest, and who warmly embraced Vasco da Gama. This priest then led them, first, into a large square in front of the palace, and then, under arches, through four spacious courts, each court being guarded by a company of Nairs.

10. At last they came to a large hall, round which were ranged rows of benches in a semicircle. A green carpet covered the floor, and the walls were hung with rich silks. The Zamorin sat in a kind of balcony, on a sofa covered with white silk and gold cloth. A heavy canopy hung above him. On his head he wore a sort of crown, on which glittered diamonds and rubies.

11. Vasco advanced up the hall. When he came in front of the Zamorin he bowed low three times, and lifted his arms towards the ceiling. The Zamorin pointed to a seat

by his side, and made signs that Vasco should sit there. At the same time the Nairs conducted the other Portuguese to the benches on either side.

12. When the company were all seated, the Zamorin's servants brought some water in basins, and offered them to the Portuguese for washing their hands. Then figs and other fruits were brought to them. As they ate, the Zamorin watched them, and seemed very much amused at their manner of eating food.

13. The fruit made the Portuguese thirsty, and they asked for some water to drink. This was brought in ewers. They were told that they must not touch the ewers with their lips, but pour the water into their hands, holding the ewers above. As they did so, some of the Portuguese choked and spluttered with the water, and others spilt it over their clothes and faces. This made the Zamorin roar with delight and slap his knees in great pleasure.

14. Then the presents which Vasco had brought were laid at the feet of the dusky monarch, who, as each rich cloth made its

appearance, the ewers, the basins, the mirror, and the chair—gazed at them with greedy delight. Vasco, through the interpreters, begged him to sit in the chair, which the Zamorin did with great good nature.

15. Turning to Vasco, he asked him to tell the courtiers what his purpose was in coming to Calicut. This Vasco refused to do, saying that he was ordered to speak only to the sovereign himself. The Zamorin accordingly led the way to an inner chamber, followed by Vasco, one or two of the higher nobles, and Nunez, Devane, and the old priest, who were to act as interpreters.

16. Vasco da Gama, when they were seated, addressed the Zamorin in these words,—

"Sire," he began, "you are great and powerful among the rulers of India, and all of them are under your feet. The King of Portugal has heard of your grandeur, and has longed to obtain your friendship and goodwill. He desires to send his ships hither with merchandise, and to trade with your people in pepper and drugs. He therefore despatched me with the presents which you see before you and by God's mercy I have come safely hither. If you, sire, give us welcome, other ships will come, when we return with the stories of your goodness, and the trade of Calicut will flourish more than ever before, because of the communication between us."

17. The Zamorin replied,—

"You shall have whatever goods you wish to put on board, and may send all your people into the town to amuse themselves, and they shall not be molested."

18. The Zamorin then questioned Vasco da Gama about his voyage, and the mishaps he had had, and asked him many things about Portugal. How far was it from India? Over what possessions did King Emmanuel rule? What were the products of the country? How many ships were there? And how large was the army?

19. Vasco answered all the questions, and said to the Zamorin—

"King Emmanuel has sent me out with the ships to discover the way to India, and to make peace with your Majesty. He commanded me not to return until I had done so. I fear that, if I should return without having obeyed his commands, he would surely order my head to be cut off."

20. It was now almost dark, and the Zamorin dismissed the Portuguese, ordering that an escort should be provided for them. When Vasco da Gama and his companions emerged into the street, they found that it was raining hard, and all their fine dresses were likely to be spoilt. Nunez told some of the men to take the captain on their backs, and so carry him across the city; but Vasco would not listen to this. Then the captain procured a horse, but, as there was no saddle, Vasco refused to mount him, and continued to go on foot through the rain.

21. When he got to the warehouse where the strangers stored their goods, he was dripping wet, so he hastened to change his rich apparel for a suit of plainer clothing. He then sat down and wrote and sent off a letter to his brother Paulo, giving him an account of his interview with the Zamorin, and his adventures in Calicut.

CHAPTER XV

Vasco da Gama a Prisoner.

1. The next day he received a gratifying token of the monarch's goodwill. The treasurer came to the warehouse with some fine stuffs worked with gold, a large porcelain jar filled with musk, and a number of curious articles, which he presented to Vasco in the Zamorin's name.

2. Meanwhile he announced that he had orders to make the warehouse more convenient for the Portuguese, and at once set some labourers to work building a spacious shed near by. When the shed—which was a rude affair, and took but a short time to put up—was finished, the treasurer had benches placed within it, where the merchants might come and sit, and barter with the Portuguese.

3. The trading now went on more

actively than before, and Vasco da Gama watched the interchange of merchandise with much curiosity and satisfaction. They were weighed and bartered during the day, and the payments were made at nightfall. In the evening the spices and drugs were conveyed by the boats to the ships.

4. Finding how much influence the treasurer and the Gozil had at court, and knowing the efforts of the Arabs to make these officers hostile to him, Vasco da Gama sent each of them some presents of satin cloth, knives, caps, and strings and branches of coral. Unfortunately he gave more to the treasurer than to the Gozil. This made the latter jealous and angry, and all the more disposed to listen to the Arabs.

5. The Arabs were very much alarmed when they saw with what favour, in spite of all their efforts, the Zamorin received the Portuguese, and the liberty which he gave them to trade in the city. They feared lest they should lose their own business altogether, and they redoubled their exertions to create enmity against the newcomers.

6. They lavished more presents on the Gozil, and finding that the captain of the guard was entrusted by the Zamorin with the duty of protecting Vasco da Gama and his retinue, they secretly went to him also, and gave him a large sum of money. They urged him to provoke the Portuguese in some way, so that they should get angry, and do something for which the Zamorin would order them to be killed, and the ships to be seized.

7. The captain of the guard happened to be poorer, and therefore more greedy of money than the other officers; and so he lent a very favourable ear to the promptings of the Arabs. He at last gave his consent to fall in with the wishes of the merchants, and prepared to put into action a plan he had formed. He was afraid to use any open violence towards the Portuguese, lest the Zamorin should punish him with the loss of his head; but he craftily devised a plan by which he hoped to entrap Vasco da Gama into some imprudent act which would give an excuse for doing him an ill turn.

8. A day or two after Vasco's visit to the

palace, the captain came to the warehouse borne in a litter, and told him that the Zamorin was about to go to his country palace, and that he desired Vasco to come and see him before he went. The Zamorin had really sent no such message, and was ignorant of what was going on.

9. Vasco da Gama, though cautious and on his guard, did not suspect any foul play. Believing that the Zamorin had sent for him, he told the captain of the guard that he would soon be ready to go with him.

10. Meanwhile the captain of the guard had taken good care that no one should tell the Zamorin of what was taking place. He placed some of his guards at the palace gates to watch all who went in and came out. He would not even allow the Gozil and the treasurer, whom he suspected of treachery, to go in to the Zamorin.

11. Before repairing, as he supposed, to the palace, Vasco da Gama gave Nunez instructions about the trading, and told him to take whatever merchandise was brought to him, whether good or bad, and to pay what was asked for it without

VASCO IS A PRISONER

question. Then he put on a red satin tunic, with a scarlet gown over it, and a red cloth cap on his head. He chose eight of the Portuguese to attend him. These were dressed in woollen jackets, and had stout sticks, instead of swords, for arms.

12. The captain of the guard ordered a very handsome litter, made of silk, ornamented with a good deal of silk fringe and embroidery, and supplied with a soft mattress, to be brought. When all was ready, Vasco da Gama got into the litter, and reclined on the mattress, and in this manner was borne away from the warehouse.

13. About noon they came to the bank of a small river. Here they saw two long boats moored at the brink. The Nair, who seemed to be in command of the rest, ordered Vasco da Gama, and three of his men, one of whom was Nunez, to get into the first boat. The other five Portuguese were then pushed into the second boat. Then the Nairs got in, and began to row the boats rapidly up the river.

14. As they passed along, they saw large

villages on either bank, the inhabitants of which flocked out, and looked at them with much curiosity and amazement. Here and there the river ran between gloomy thickets, now and then broad sandy plains stretched away from the banks. The boat carrying Vasco da Gama soon left the other far behind. Once, when he turned round, he perceived that the latter was quite out of sight. He was angry at this, but the Nairs paid no attention to him, and rowed steadily on.

15. By-and-by they came to a small hamlet, where there were several low, thatched houses. The boat stopped near the bank, and waited while some rice was cooked. Neither Vasco nor his companions were allowed to land. The rice was handed in to them, but Vasco was so angry and amazed at his treatment that he would not touch it.

16. The boat sped on, and did not stop again till darkness fell. Then the prisoners were taken on shore, and shut up in a small house for the night. Very early in the morning Vasco da Gama was suddenly

wakened by a Nair, who told him that the captain of the guard had arrived, and wanted to see him. To put on his cloak and sally out took but a moment. They would let none of his men accompany him, except an interpreter. As he went away, Vasco warned his companions to be discreet, and to say or do nothing, whatever happened. Meanwhile, the other boat had come, and the Portuguese, who had been brought in it, were lodged in a hut close by that one in which Vasco had spent the night.

CHAPTER XVI.

Vasco da Gama Set Free.

1. Vasco spent a lonely and sleepless night in the solitude of the new prison, and was relieved when, in the morning, he was at last led to the captain of the guard. The captain was sitting on a couch. When Vasco entered, he neither offered him a seat nor spoke to him. A surly frown was on his dark face. In a moment or two Joan Nunez was brought in to interpret what was said.

2. The captain of the guard then spoke in an insolent tone, through Nunez, to Vasco da Gama.

"We have heard from Mombasa," he said, "that you Portuguese are robbers, going about the seas plundering. The Zamorin has ordered that your ships should be taken, and all of you kept prisoners till you confess the truth. Now, you had better tell me the truth, and I will go and relate it to the Zamorin."

3. "If you will conduct me to the Zamorin," replied Vasco, "I will tell him the truth; but I will not tell you anything."

The captain of the guard got up in a great temper, and cried out,—

"Why won't you tell it to me?"

Vasco remained silent.

4. The captain kept on asking questions; but Vasco would not open his lips. Then the enraged officer ordered the Nairs to take him away, and to shut him in a house by himself. He next tried to get something out of Nunez, but this shrewd fellow evaded his questions, and he, too, was again imprisoned.

5. Finding that he could not make Vasco or any other of the Portuguese angry (which he had intended when he took them prisoners and brought them away), and fearing to do them any violence lest the Zamorin (who was ignorant of all these things, being away at his country house)

should order his head to be cut off, the captain of the guard was greatly puzzled to decide what course to take.

6. At last he resolved that he would try to regain Vasco's goodwill, and get out of the scrape as best he could. He had obtained all the money from the Arabs he could hope for, and his interest now was to shield himself from the Zamorin's anger.

7. The next day, therefore, he sent for Vasco, and told him that the Zamorin had made up his mind that all the merchandise of the ships should be sent ashore to the factory; and that then, in four days, he would allow him to take in his cargo of spices and drugs; after that, the ships should sail without delay.

8. Vasco replied that he would obey the Zamorin's commands, but that in order to do so, it was necessary to send a messenger to the ships. The captain of the guard then sent for the rest of the Portuguese to come to their captain. When they saw Vasco they gathered round him and shouted for joy. They had been haunted with the fear that he might have been murdered.

9. But Vasco da Gama's troubles were not yet over. The captain of the guard conducted him back to the city, and lodged him on one of the quays at some distance from the warehouse.

From this new prison Vasco was allowed to send a message to his brother Paulo. He apprised him of all that had happened, and that he was still a prisoner; told him to send the goods ashore; warned him to see that the hostages did not escape; and, if Paulo found that Vasco was not released, to order back Diaz the agent, and allow no one to go on shore.

10. He attempted to get his release and go to the "San Raphael," but this the captain of the guard would not permit. Vasco subdued his anger as best he could, and this time sent a very different message to Paulo.

"Tell him," said he to the messenger, "that I do not think they intend to set me free, no matter how many goods are sent on shore. Beg him, for God's sake, if he sees that they will not release me, to send the hostages on shore, and then at once set sail.

If they do not allow me to go when the hostages come, then let Paulo return at once to Portugal, and tell the King what has happened. It is of little matter if I am killed, but it is of great importance that the news of the discovery of India should be carried back to Portugal.

11. When Paulo received this message, he warmly declared that he would not go away without Vasco, but would risk his life and those of all the men in the attempt to save him, as they were all ready to die for their captain.

"Let the captain of the guard beware," said he, "for I will make war and destroy every ship in the port."

12. Paulo ordered that no more goods should be sent on shore, and sent word to Vasco that he should stay to defend him.

The captain of the guard, angry that the goods were not sent (for he expected to get a share of them himself), thought it time to speak to the Zamorin, and, while concealing his harsh treatment of Vasco, to try and rouse his anger against him.

13. He told the Zamorin that the Portu-

guese had not only refused to send any more goods on shore, but were threatening to burn the city and the ships. The Arab merchants added their persuasions to those of the captain of the guard. Their story so enraged the Zamorin, that he ordered that their goods at the warehouse should be seized, and that Vasco and his comrades should at once be put to death.

14. The captain of the guard was hurrying away joyfully to obey this command, when the chief priest, a venerable man, told him to stop. Turning to the Zamorin, the priest said,—

"Sire, do not do this thing. Even if what the captain of the guard says is true, the Portuguese have as yet done no harm, but, like good people, have been very mild and peaceable. Do not execute your will until they have shown a disposition to do some injury."

15. This wise advice was adopted by the Zamorin, after a fierce debate with the Arabs.

Only one way to secure the release of Vasco da Gama remained to Paulo. This was to send the hostages ashore, and to trust to this generous act, and to their persuasions with the Zamorin, to obtain Vasco's freedom.

16. The hostages, who had been kindly and generously treated by the Portuguese, willingly agreed to use every effort to accomplish this. They were accordingly sent off in a boat, having received presents of satin cloth, red caps, and knives.

17. They hastened to the palace, and, kneeling before the Zamorin, revealed to him the whole story of Vasco's imprisonment, and the treatment he had received at the hands of the captain of the guard. They besought him to set Vasco free, and declared that, if he did not, they would kill themselves, as they had staked their heads on the Zamorin's good faith. They begged him to reflect what dishonour and bad reputation he would incur if Vasco met with foul play, and assured him that the Portuguese meant no harm to him or the city.

18. The Zamorin was amazed and angry to hear of the captain of the guard's con-

duct, and at once resolved to make all the reparation in his power. Sending for Vasco da Gama, who was wholly in the dark, and did not know what was coming next, the Zamorin frankly begged his pardon for what had occurred, and declared he would severely punish those who had been guilty of it. He told Vasco that he might go to his ships as soon as he pleased. As he spoke, he gave him a large jewel set with rubies and pearls in token of his regret and goodwill.

19. Vasco da Gama lost no time in taking advantage of his freedom. Attended by his Portuguese comrades and a large company of Nairs, he hastened to the quay, got into a boat, and set out for the "San Raphael." Just as the boat was pushing off, Monsayde ran up and jumped into it, Vasco willingly consenting that he should go to the ship with him.

20. When Vasco appeared on deck, his brother rushed forward and fervently embraced him. The sailors gathered round him, and many of them wept for joy at seeing their beloved captain again. That

night there was much feasting and merriment on board the ships.

21. The next morning a fair wind sprang up. Taking a last look at the minarets, quays, and the streets of Calicut, the Portuguese weighed anchor, and sailed slowly out into the open sea.

CHAPTER XVII.

Welcome Home.

1. It was late in November when the "San Gabriel" floated out of Calicut harbour. Vasco had already been absent from Portugal a year and seven months. On the return voyage he called at Cananor, on the coast of India, where Devane, the faithful Moor, decided to remain.

2. From thence the Portuguese proceeded to Goa, a large place many leagues north of Calicut. Here an attempt was made to capture the vessels, but the Goanese were driven off by a night attack.

3. The Indian Ocean was recrossed in four weeks, and the coast of Africa was greeted by the crews with wild demonstrations of joy. Early in January, 1499, Vasco da Gama was once more anchored

at Melinda, and received a hearty welcome from the King.

4. After a stay of twelve days, during which the vessels were supplied with fresh water and provisions, the voyage was resumed. A call was made at Zanzibar and also at San Blas. Then the Cape of Good Hope was rounded, and the vessels made for the Cape Verde Islands, which they reached in August.

5. Soon after passing the Cape, Paulo da Gama had been taken sick. He was very ill when the ships reached the Cape Verde Islands and was tenderly carried on shore, where he died the next day. His grief-stricken brother followed him to the grave, attended by all the Portuguese in deep mourning.

6. When Vasco set sail from the Cape Verde Islands his heart was oppressed with grief at his brother's death. The exultation that he might have felt to think that, within a few days, he would be received with wild rejoicing and highest honours by his King and countrymen, was now obscured by the gloom that overshadowed his heart.

7. The news of his successful voyage reached Lisbon before him. The King was also informed of Paulo da Gama's death, and Vasco's intense grief at the event. He was ready to receive the explorers at Lisbon, and fully prepared to confer on them such rewards and honours as he felt their intrepid courage and great achievement deserved.

8. The King had not long to wait for the arrival of the vessels. A day or two afterwards it was announced they had entered the mouth of the river, and were fast approaching the bar at Lisbon. The news quickly spread from the palace to the city and the harbour. All Lisbon turned out, and hurried in multitudes down to the quays.

9. The harbour was full of ships and boats. Ere long they all appeared, gaily decked out with flags and streamers, while the sailors crowded out on the decks in their best suits. The people, also dressed in holiday attire, flocked through the narrow streets and across the broad squares. The city hummed with excited voices and shouts of joy.

10. On the principal quay was a large

building with a balcony, over which hung a canopy; it was called the "House of Mines." Hither the King, attended by the court, came, and seats were provided for the royal folk on the balcony.

11. Presently the booming of cannon was heard in the distance. It came nearer and nearer, and now was echoed by the cannon on the ships in harbour. Then two vessels were seen slowly floating in an open space that the ships made for them in the centre of the harbour. These, too, sent out deafening volleys, and from their mastheads fluttered the royal ensign and the flag of Portugal. They were the "San Raphael" and the "San Gabriel."

12. Vasco da Gama could be seen standing on the quarter-deck of the "San Raphael," wearing a plumed hat, and waving his hands on this side and on that. Below, on the main deck, the cross-bowmen, sailors, and officers, with whom mingled the dark Melinda pilots in their Oriental costume, huddled together at the side of the ship, and gazed eagerly towards the dear and familiar shore.

13. What a thrilling scene it was! How the hearts of the weary wanderers must have bounded to behold each familiar object—the spires of the churches, the well-remembered streets and squares, the easily-recognised hills and cliffs, the spots where were their homes! And then how they must have strained their eyes through the crowd on the quays, in the hope that they might make out the beloved forms of dear ones left so long behind. Soon, indeed, they would be locked in the embraces of parents, wives, and children, or would be bowed with grief at the news of the death of beloved relatives and friends.

14. As Vasco went along to the House of Mines, the people observed that his beard had grown very long and that his face was pale and sad. They shouted and cheered frantically as the hero passed between their ranks, and blessings were showered on him on every hand.

When he ascended to the balcony, King Emmanuel, as a mark of peculiar favour, rose from his chair to greet him. Vasco da Gama kneeled and kissed the royal hand, but King Emmanuel immediately raised him and warmly embraced him.

"Sire," said Vasco, "all my hardships have now come to a happy end, since I am once more brought into the presence of your Majesty, as I have always prayed."

15. "May your coming be fortunate," returned King Emmanuel; "your return fills me with pride and happiness, and, since God has been pleased to bring you back in safety, He has reserved you for the rewards which your heroism deserves. But, for my sake, be consoled for the death of your brother."

16. The King now descended, mounted his horse, and with Vasco da Gama riding at his side, and the courtiers following, a dazzling group, repaired to the palace. Here he brought Vasco to his fair young queen, whose hand Vasco kissed, while she received him with gracious welcome.

17. Meanwhile a touching scene was being enacted on the quays. The sailors and other companions of Vasco da Gama on his voyage had come on shore, and were being overwhelmed with the joyfully tearful caresses of their friends and families. Their

weather beaten faces quivered with emotion as the dear wife, the fair young child, and aged mother were fondly folded to their bosoms.

18. Troops of old friends and cronies crowded round them and hugged them, and bore them away in triumph up the zigzag streets to their longed-for homes, where happy feasts awaited them. Each man was a wonderful hero to his friends. He had braved unheard-of perils, and had seen such strange things and people as nobody had imagined existed on earth. That night many a group sat round the homely hearths of Lisbon, and listened to the marvellous tales of the East which the wayfarers told.

19. The voyage of Vasco da Gama had lasted from the 25th of March, 1497, to the 18th of September, 1499—a period of about two years and six months. He had started with one hundred men, and returned with about one-third of that number. His frail little vessels had been new when he set out. When he got back they were worn and seemed old, and were no longer fit for such hard work.

20. It remained to settle up accounts, to pay the men, to distribute the cargo, and to dispense the rewards that had been so bravely won. The crossbow men were generously paid in money, and were allowed, besides, to carry ten pounds of spices each home to their wives. The heirs of the dead sailors were paid their wages, and shares of the goods. Each master and pilot received, besides his wages, a share of every drug that the ships carried.

21. Nicholas Coello received a large sum of money, a quantity of the spices and drugs, a share of the presents, and was made a lord of the royal household. To Vasco da Gama, besides the noble title of "Don," King Emmanuel gave a grant of a yearly sum of two hundred ducats to spend in spices from India, which he should bring in duty free, besides a pension of about a thousand dollars a year, which was then worth about as much as two thousand pounds is worth now. He gave him permission to wear the royal arms. He made him lord of the village of Sinis, in which Don Vasco was born.

22. Thus ended the famous first voyage of

Vasco da Gama; and thus he was received, when, after so many dangers and adventures, he at last returned to his native Portugal. His fame rapidly spread through Portugal and all Europe. He was hailed as the rival of Columbus, and the kings envied the good fortune of King Emmanuel in having so valiant and persevering a navigator. The greatest of Portuguese poets celebrated his heroic character and deeds in a poem which still preserves his memory; and he became the pride and idol of his countrymen.